TRAGEDY! TALES FROM THE TITANIC

Stories of Survival

BY SARAH EASON
ILLUSTRATED BY ALEK SOTIROVSKI

BEAR CLAW

Credits

20, © Wikimedia Commons/Thomas Barker; 21b, © Wikimedia Commons/Library of Congress; 21r, © Wikimedia Commons/J.W. Barker; 22t, © Wikimedia Commons; 22b, © Wikimedia Commons/Library of Congress; 23, © Wikimedia Commons.

Editor: Jennifer Sanderson
Proofreader: Katie Dicker
Designer: Paul Myerscough
Picture Researcher: Katie Dicker

Bearport Publishing Company Product Development Team

Publisher: Jen Jenson; Director of Product Development: Spencer Brinker; Managing Editor: Allison Juda; Editor: Cole Nelson; Associate Editor: Naomi Reich; Associate Editor: Tiana Tran; Art Director: Colin O'Dea; Designer: Kim Jones; Designer: Kayla Eggert; Product Development Specialist: Owen Hamlin

Statement on Usage of Generative Artificial Intelligence

Bearport Publishing remains committed to publishing high-quality nonfiction books. Therefore, we restrict the use of generative AI to ensure accuracy of all text and visual components pertaining to a book's subject. See BearportPublishing.com for details.

A Note on Graphic Narrative Nonfiction

This graphic story is a dramatization based on true events. It is intended to give the reader a sense of the narrative rather than a presentation of actual details as they occurred.

Library of Congress Cataloging-in-Publication Data

Names: Eason, Sarah, author. | Sotirovski, Aleksandar, illustrator.
Title: Stories of survival / Sarah Eason ; Illustrated by Alek Sotirovski.
Description: Bear claw books. | Minneapolis, Minnesota : Bearport
   Publishing Company, 2025. | Series: Tragedy! Tales from the Titanic |
   Includes bibliographical references and index.
Identifiers: LCCN 2024034182 (print) | LCCN 2024034183 (ebook) | ISBN
   9798892328579 (library binding) | ISBN 9798892329477 (paperback) | ISBN
   9798892328647 (ebook)
Subjects: LCSH: Titanic (Steamship)--Juvenile literature. | Titanic
   (Steamship)--Comic books, strips, etc. | Survival at sea--Great
   Britain--History--20th century--Juvenile literature. | Survival at
   sea--Great Britain--History--20th century--Juvenile literature. | Ocean
   liners--Great Britain--History--20th century--Juvenile literature. |
   Ocean liners--Great Britain--History--20th century--Comic books, strips,
   etc. | Shipwrecks--North Atlantic Ocean--History--20th century--Juvenile
   literature. | Shipwrecks--North Atlantic Ocean--History--20th
   century--Comic books, strips, etc. | Graphic novels.
Classification: LCC G530.T6 E32 2025 (print) | LCC G530.T6 (ebook) | DDC
   910.9163/4--dc23/eng20240724
LC record available at https://lccn.loc.gov/2024034182
LC ebook record available at https://lccn.loc.gov/2024034183

Copyright © 2025 Bearport Publishing Company. All rights reserved. No part of this publication may be reproduced in whole or in part, stored in any retrieval system, or transmitted in any form or by any means, electronic, mechanical, photocopying, recording, or otherwise, without written permission from the publisher.

For more information, write to Bearport Publishing, 5357 Penn Avenue South, Minneapolis, MN 55419.

Contents

CHAPTER 1
Tragedy and Triumph **4**

CHAPTER 2
Against the Odds **6**

CHAPTER 3
Big Decisions **10**

CHAPTER 4
Rescued **16**

Lifesaving Measures 20
More *Titanic* Stories 22
Glossary 23
Index 24
Read More 24
Learn More Online 24

CHAPTER 1

Tragedy and Triumph

After the famous **ocean liner** *Titanic* hit an iceberg and sank, news of the disaster quickly spread around the world.

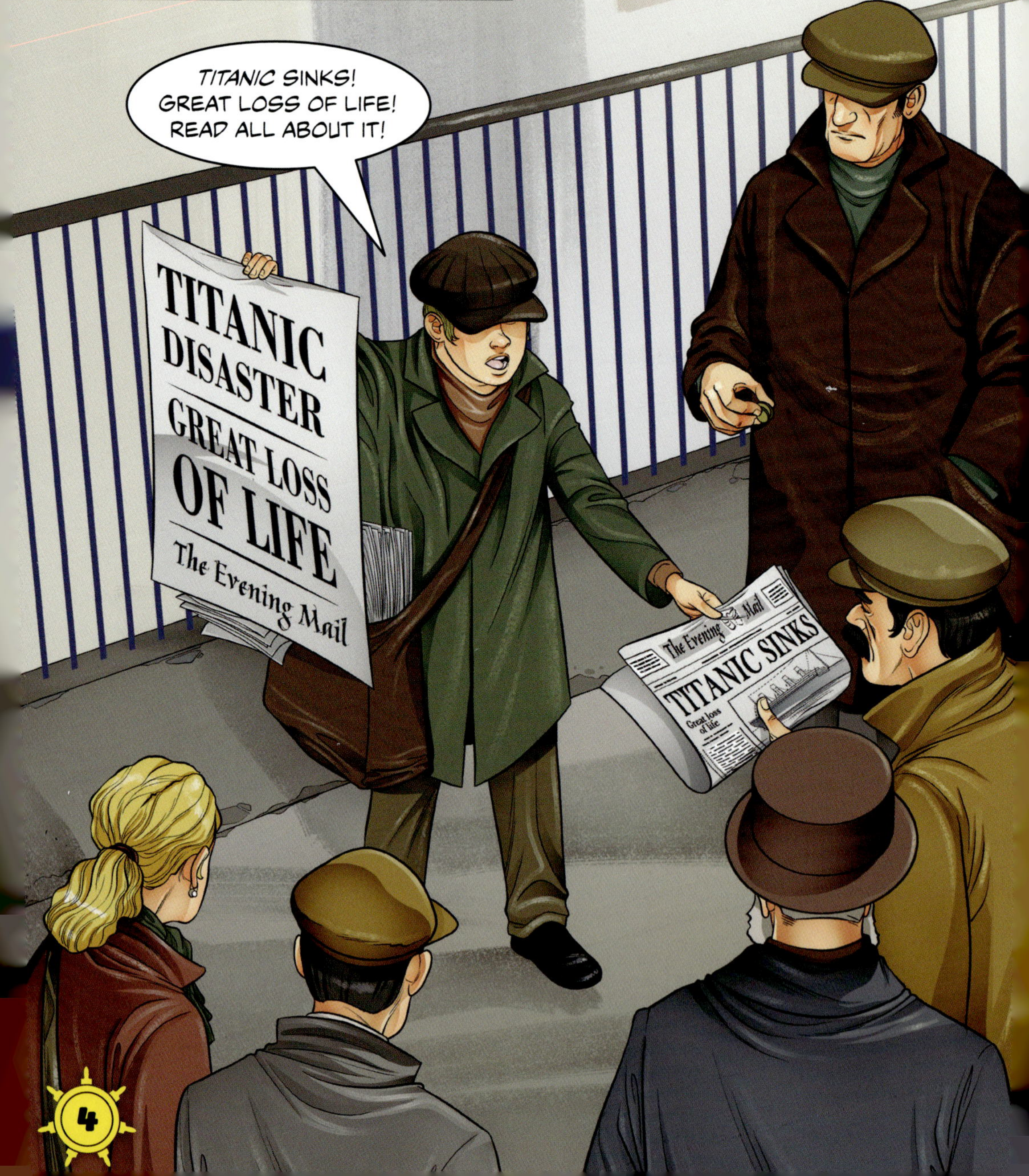

TITANIC SINKS! GREAT LOSS OF LIFE! READ ALL ABOUT IT!
TITANIC DISASTER
GREAT LOSS OF LIFE
The Evening Mail
The Evening Mail
TITANIC SINKS
Great loss of life

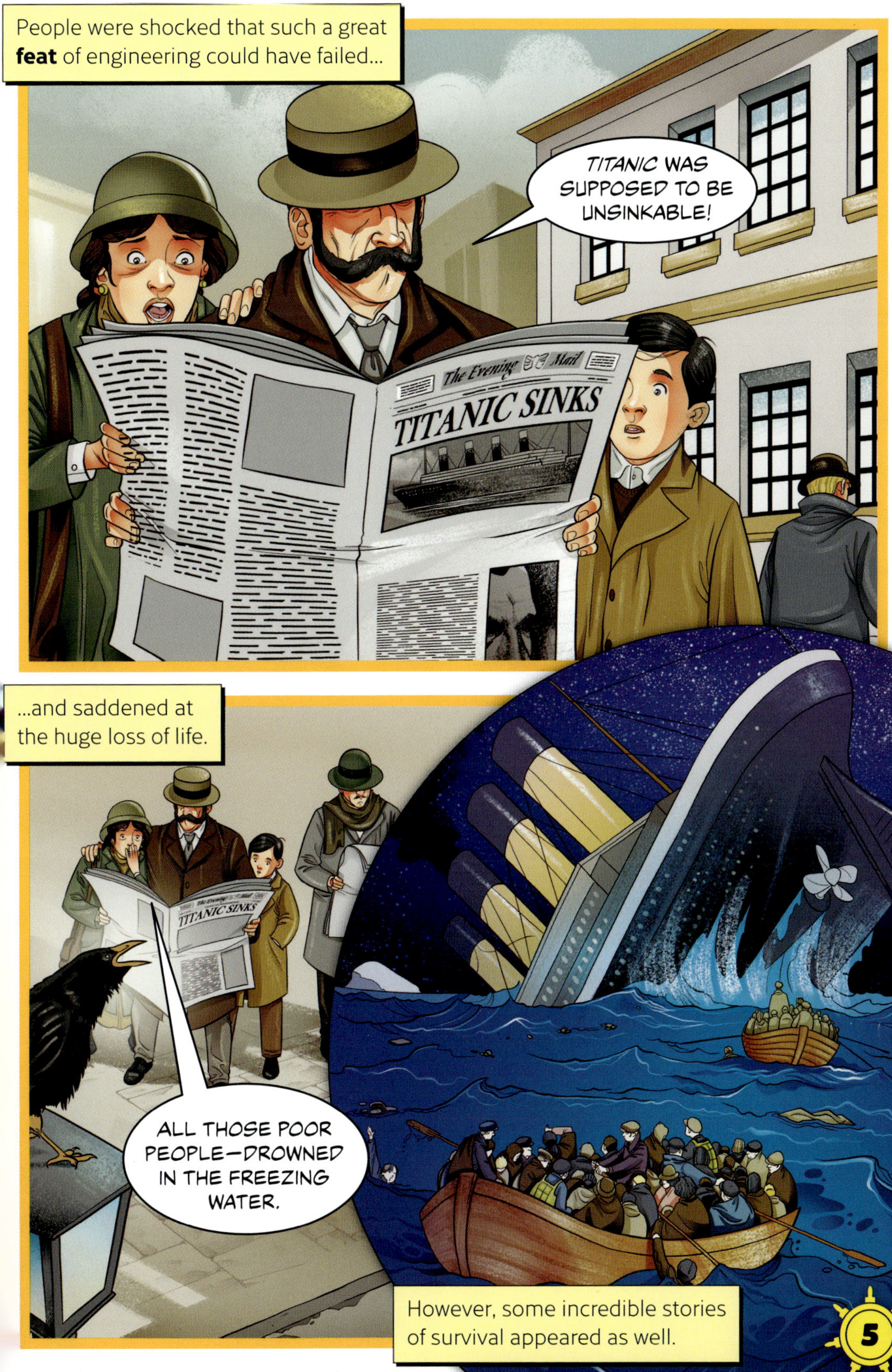
People were shocked that such a great **feat** of engineering could have failed...
TITANIC WAS SUPPOSED TO BE UNSINKABLE!
The Evening Mail
TITANIC SINKS
...and saddened at the huge loss of life.
TITANIC SINKS
ALL THOSE POOR PEOPLE—DROWNED IN THE FREEZING WATER.
However, some incredible stories of survival appeared as well.

CHAPTER 2

Against the Odds

First-class passenger Jack Thayer was on *Titanic* during the **fateful** voyage. The 17-year-old boarded the RMS *Titanic* in Cherbourg, France, along with his parents.

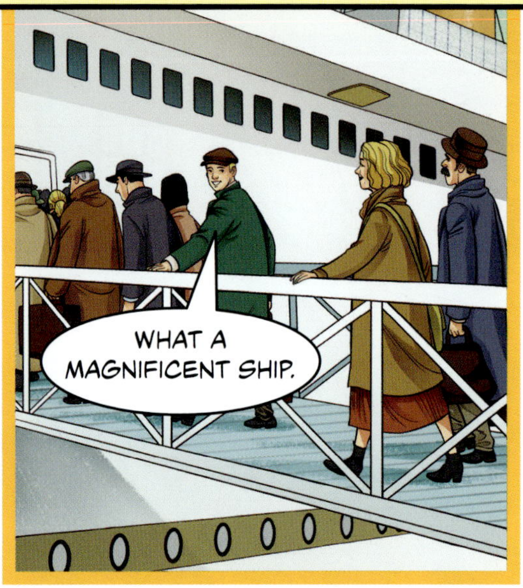
WHAT A MAGNIFICENT SHIP.

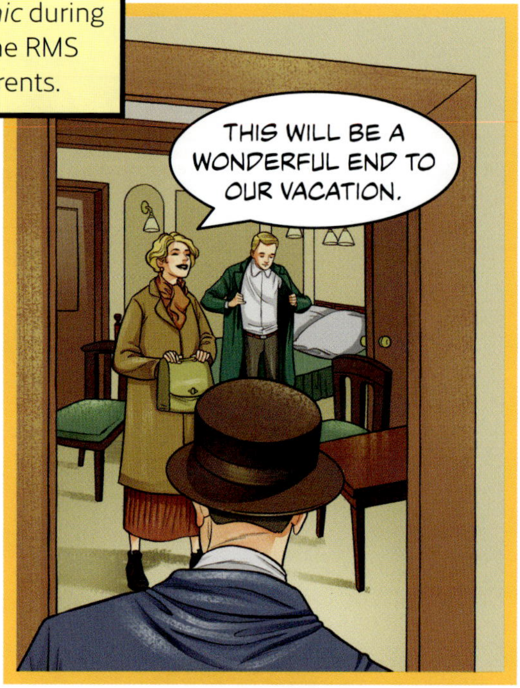
THIS WILL BE A WONDERFUL END TO OUR VACATION.

Late in the evening on April 14, 1912, Jack noticed that the ship had stopped. He went to the **deck** to find out why.

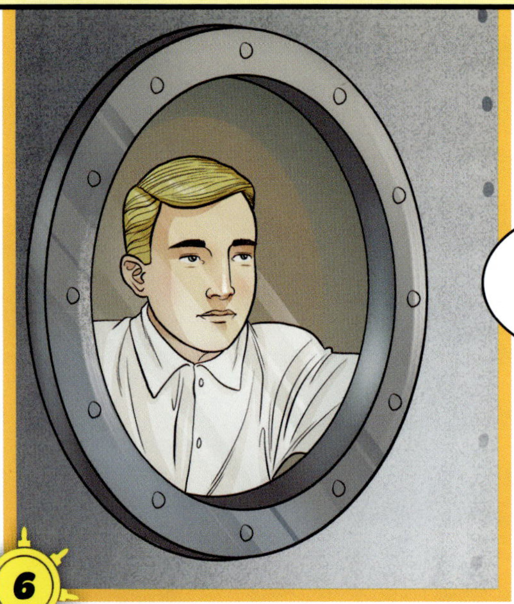

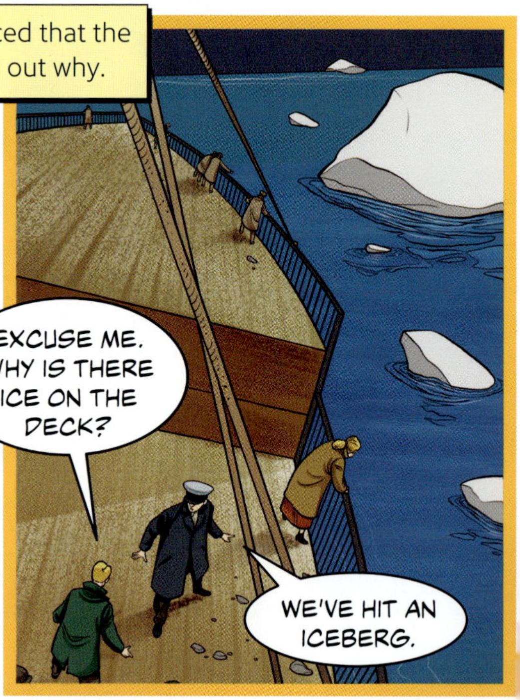
EXCUSE ME. WHY IS THERE ICE ON THE DECK?
WE'VE HIT AN ICEBERG.

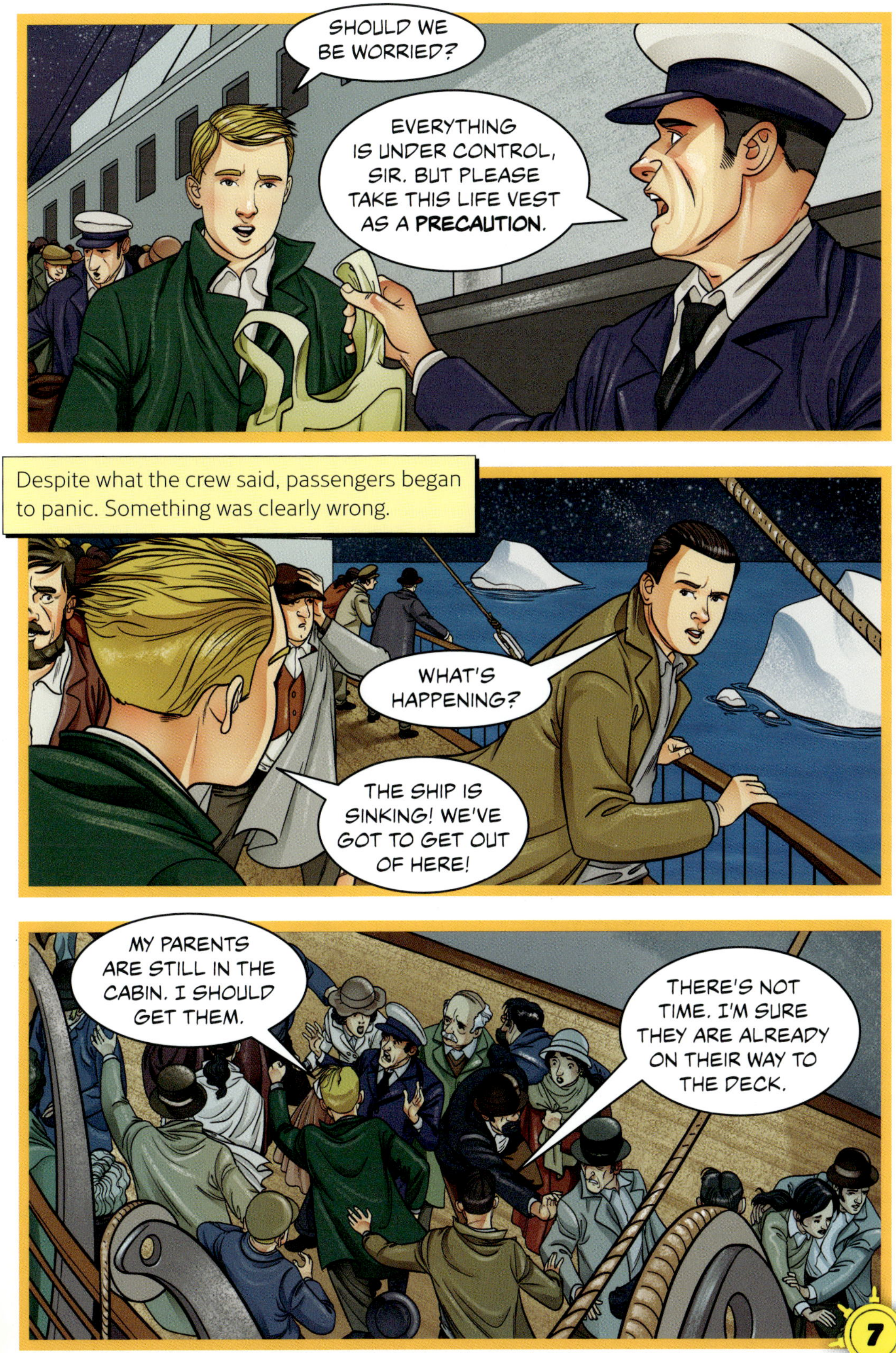
SHOULD WE BE WORRIED?
EVERYTHING IS UNDER CONTROL, SIR. BUT PLEASE TAKE THIS LIFE VEST AS A **PRECAUTION**.
Despite what the crew said, passengers began to panic. Something was clearly wrong.
WHAT'S HAPPENING?
THE SHIP IS SINKING! WE'VE GOT TO GET OUT OF HERE!
MY PARENTS ARE STILL IN THE CABIN. I SHOULD GET THEM.
THERE'S NOT TIME. I'M SURE THEY ARE ALREADY ON THEIR WAY TO THE DECK.

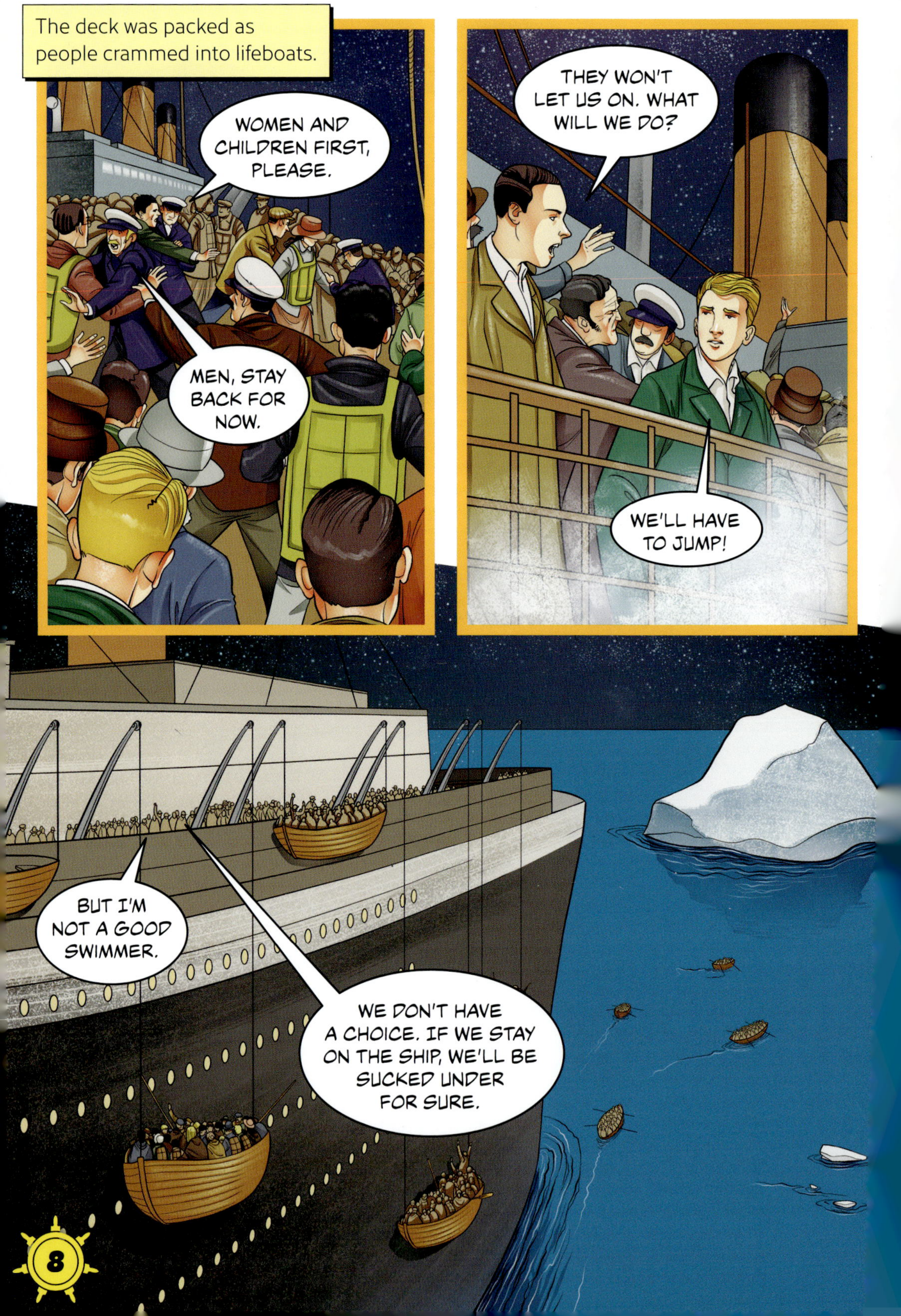

The deck was packed as people crammed into lifeboats.
WOMEN AND CHILDREN FIRST, PLEASE.
MEN, STAY BACK FOR NOW.
THEY WON'T LET US ON. WHAT WILL WE DO?
WE'LL HAVE TO JUMP!
BUT I'M NOT A GOOD SWIMMER.
WE DON'T HAVE A CHOICE. IF WE STAY ON THE SHIP, WE'LL BE SUCKED UNDER FOR SURE.

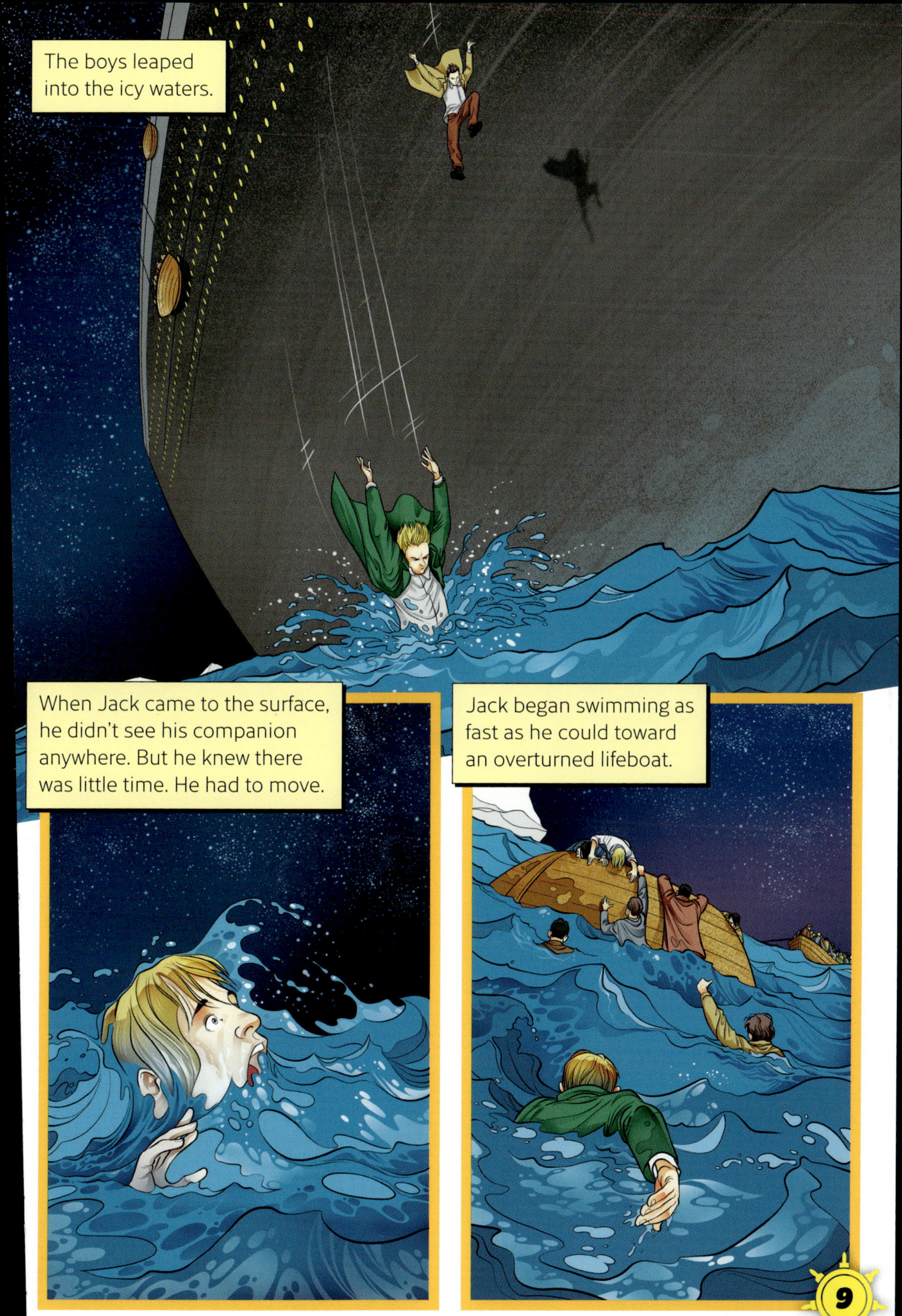
The boys leaped into the icy waters.
When Jack came to the surface, he didn't see his companion anywhere. But he knew there was little time. He had to move.
Jack began swimming as fast as he could toward an overturned lifeboat.

CHAPTER 3

Big Decisions

As the boat began tipping, families had to make a horrible choice.

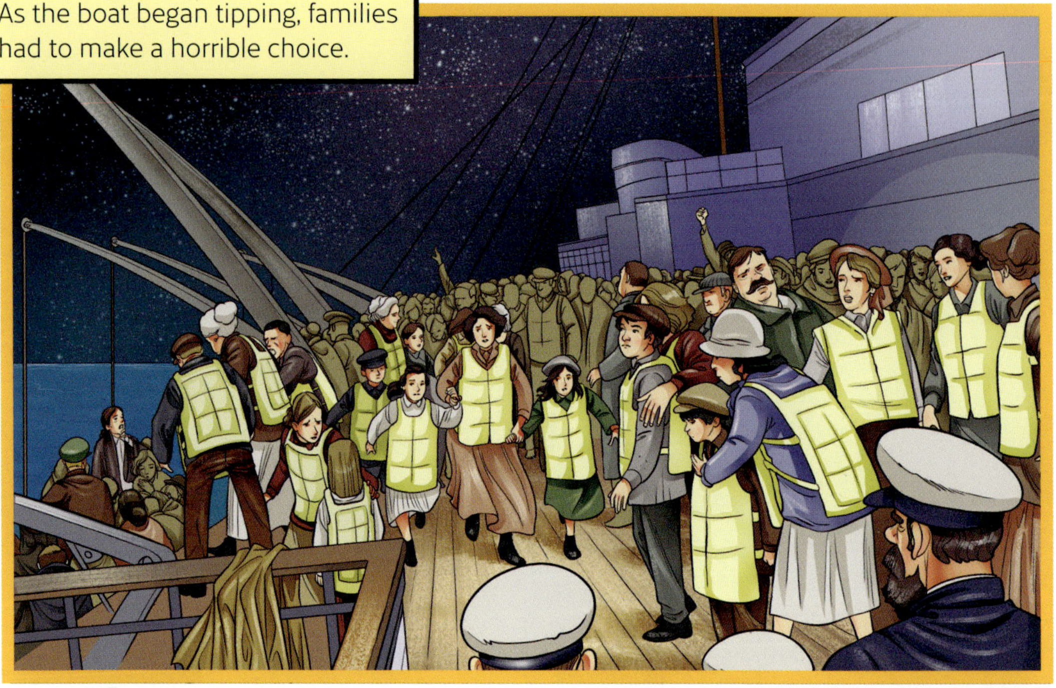

Wealthy passengers Isidor and Ida Straus were with other first-class guests lining up at the lifeboats.

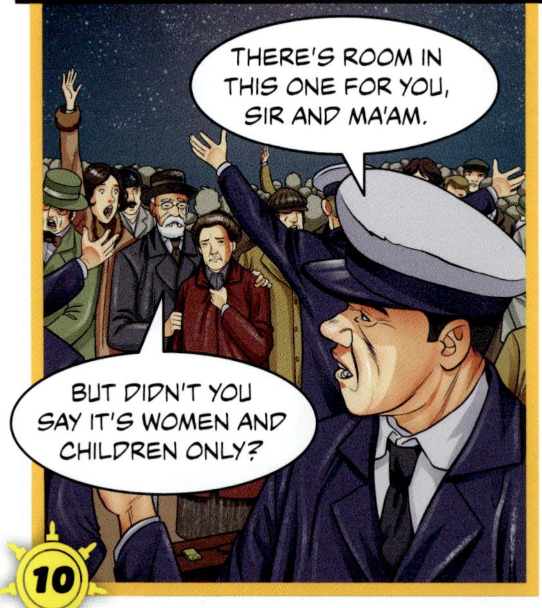
THERE'S ROOM IN THIS ONE FOR YOU, SIR AND MA'AM.
BUT DIDN'T YOU SAY IT'S WOMEN AND CHILDREN ONLY?

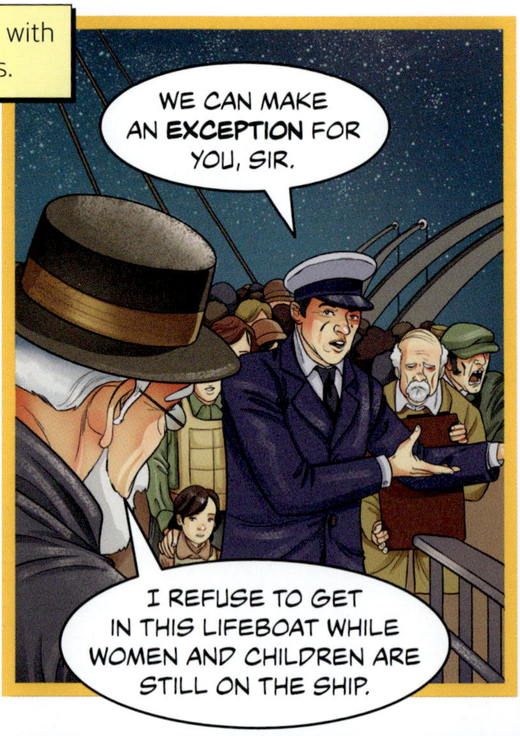
WE CAN MAKE AN **EXCEPTION** FOR YOU, SIR.
I REFUSE TO GET IN THIS LIFEBOAT WHILE WOMEN AND CHILDREN ARE STILL ON THE SHIP.

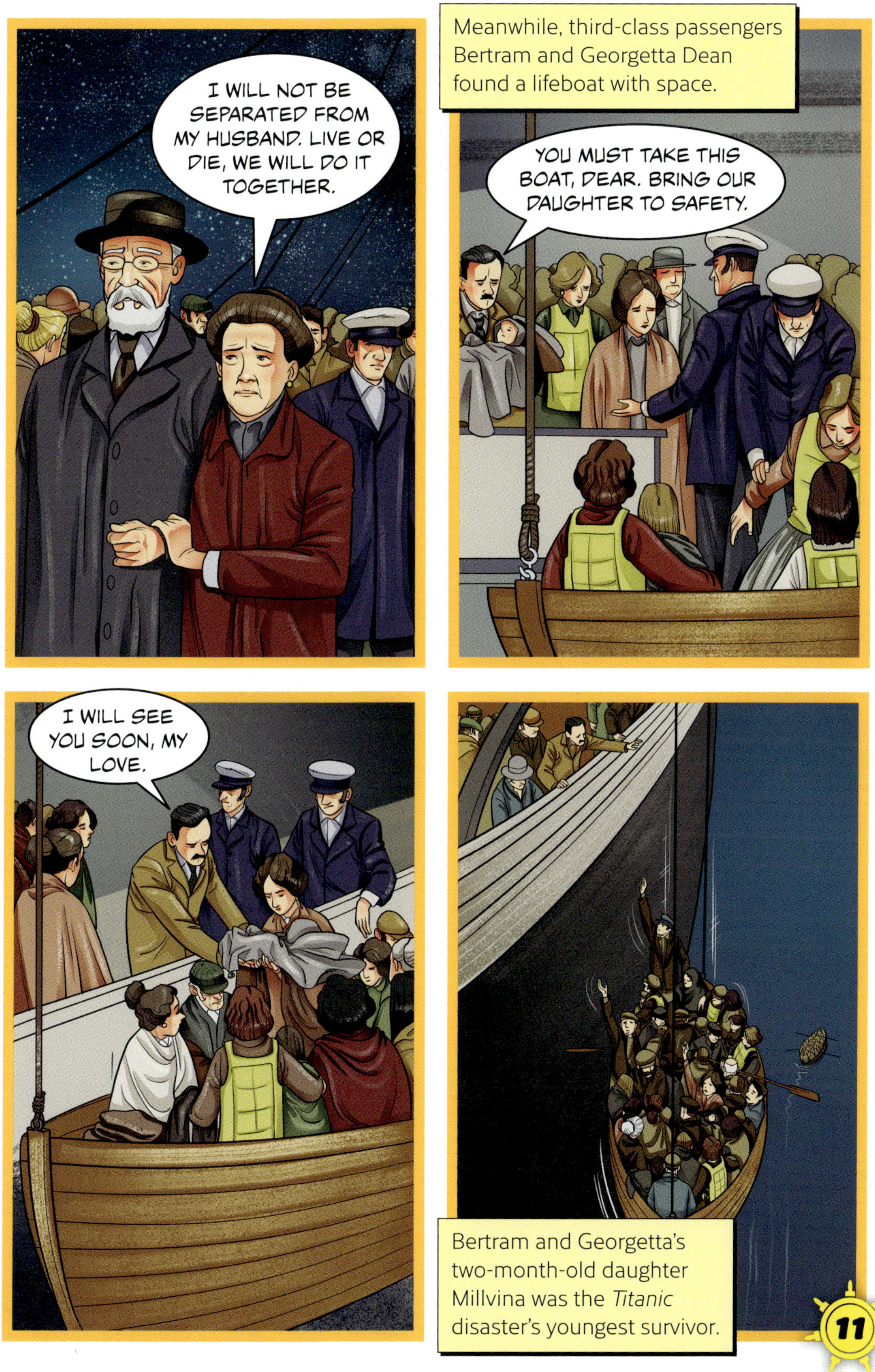
I WILL NOT BE SEPARATED FROM MY HUSBAND. LIVE OR DIE, WE WILL DO IT TOGETHER.
Meanwhile, third-class passengers Bertram and Georgetta Dean found a lifeboat with space.
YOU MUST TAKE THIS BOAT, DEAR. BRING OUR DAUGHTER TO SAFETY.
I WILL SEE YOU SOON, MY LOVE.
Bertram and Georgetta's two-month-old daughter Millvina was the *Titanic* disaster's youngest survivor.

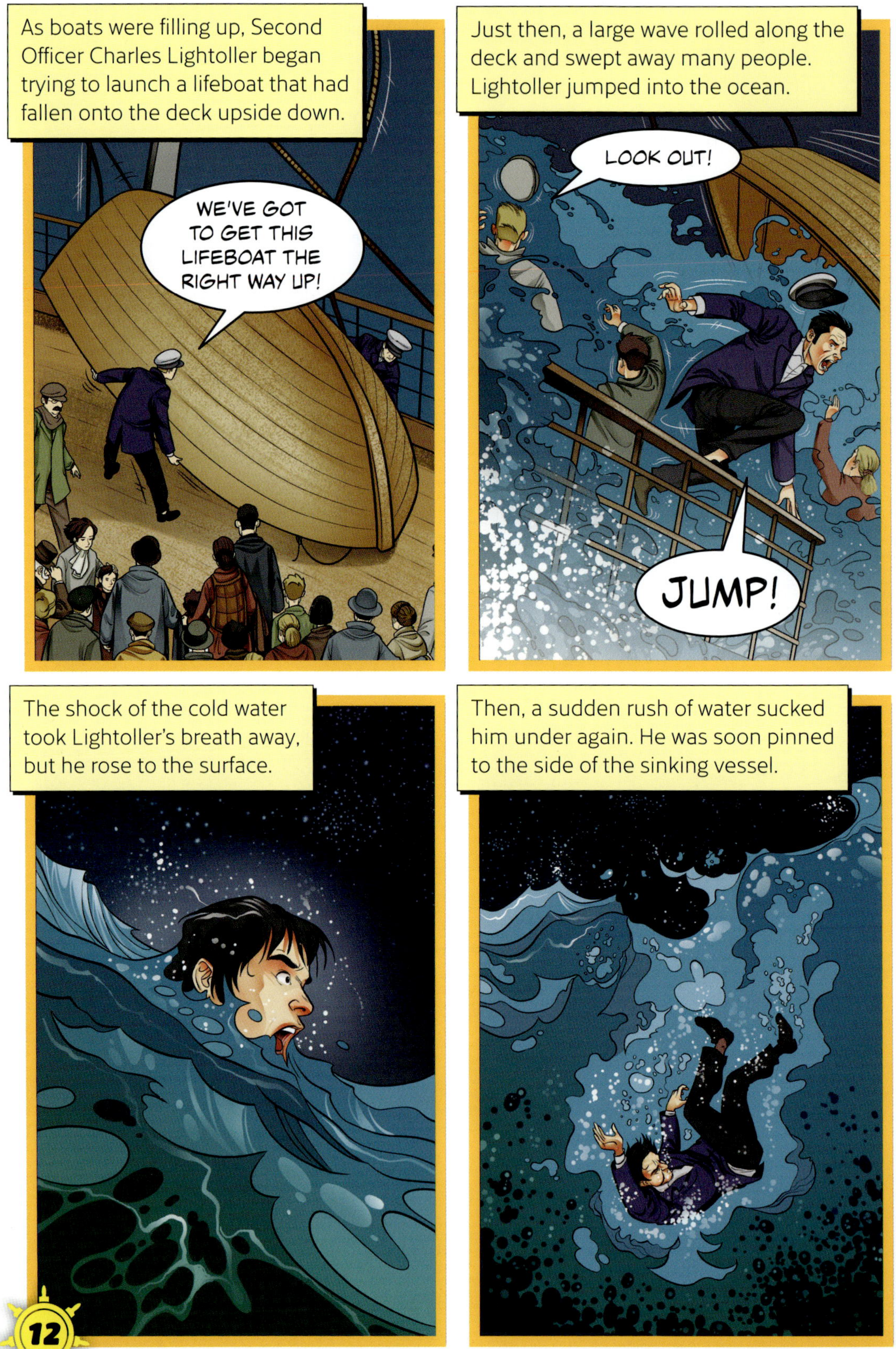
As boats were filling up, Second Officer Charles Lightoller began trying to launch a lifeboat that had fallen onto the deck upside down.
WE'VE GOT TO GET THIS LIFEBOAT THE RIGHT WAY UP!
Just then, a large wave rolled along the deck and swept away many people. Lightoller jumped into the ocean.
LOOK OUT!
JUMP!
The shock of the cold water took Lightoller's breath away, but he rose to the surface.
Then, a sudden rush of water sucked him under again. He was soon pinned to the side of the sinking vessel.

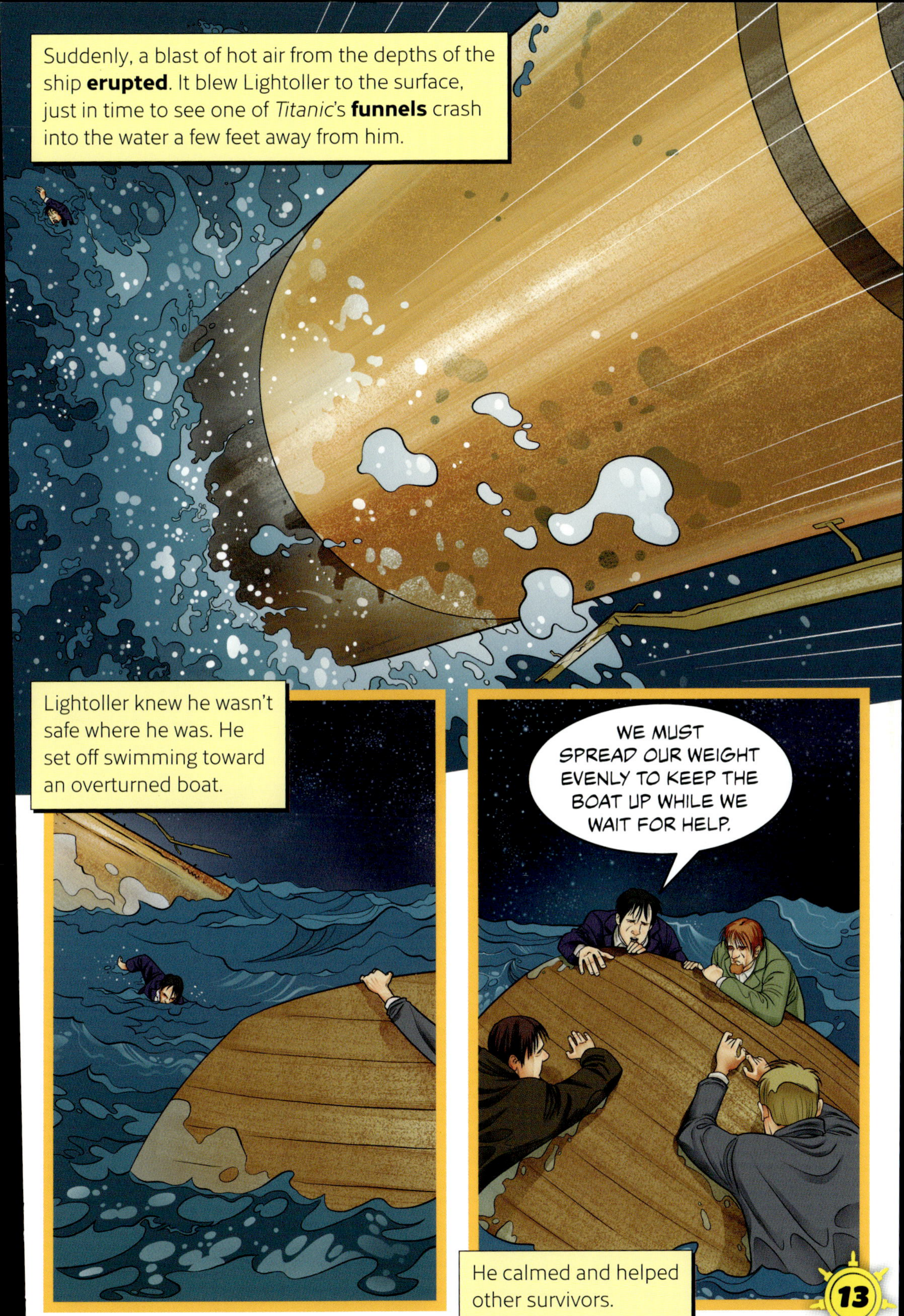
Suddenly, a blast of hot air from the depths of the ship erupted. It blew Lightoller to the surface, just in time to see one of Titanic's funnels crash into the water a few feet away from him.
Lightoller knew he wasn't safe where he was. He set off swimming toward an overturned boat.
WE MUST SPREAD OUR WEIGHT EVENLY TO KEEP THE BOAT UP WHILE WE WAIT FOR HELP.
He calmed and helped other survivors.

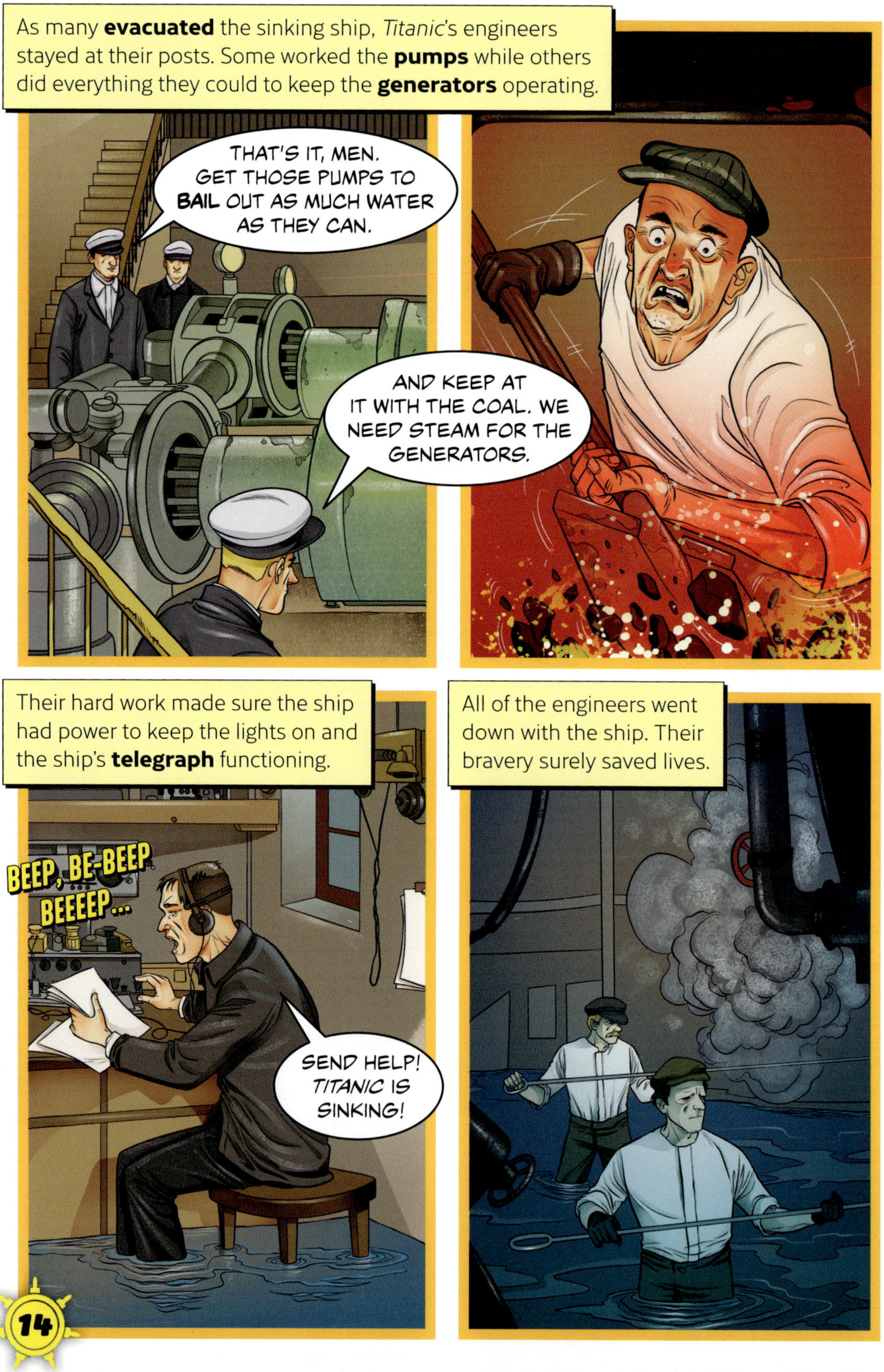
As many **evacuated** the sinking ship, *Titanic*'s engineers stayed at their posts. Some worked the **pumps** while others did everything they could to keep the **generators** operating.
THAT'S IT, MEN. GET THOSE PUMPS TO **BAIL** OUT AS MUCH WATER AS THEY CAN.
AND KEEP AT IT WITH THE COAL. WE NEED STEAM FOR THE GENERATORS.
Their hard work made sure the ship had power to keep the lights on and the ship's **telegraph** functioning.
BEEP, BE-BEEP BEEEEP...
SEND HELP! *TITANIC* IS SINKING!
All of the engineers went down with the ship. Their bravery surely saved lives.

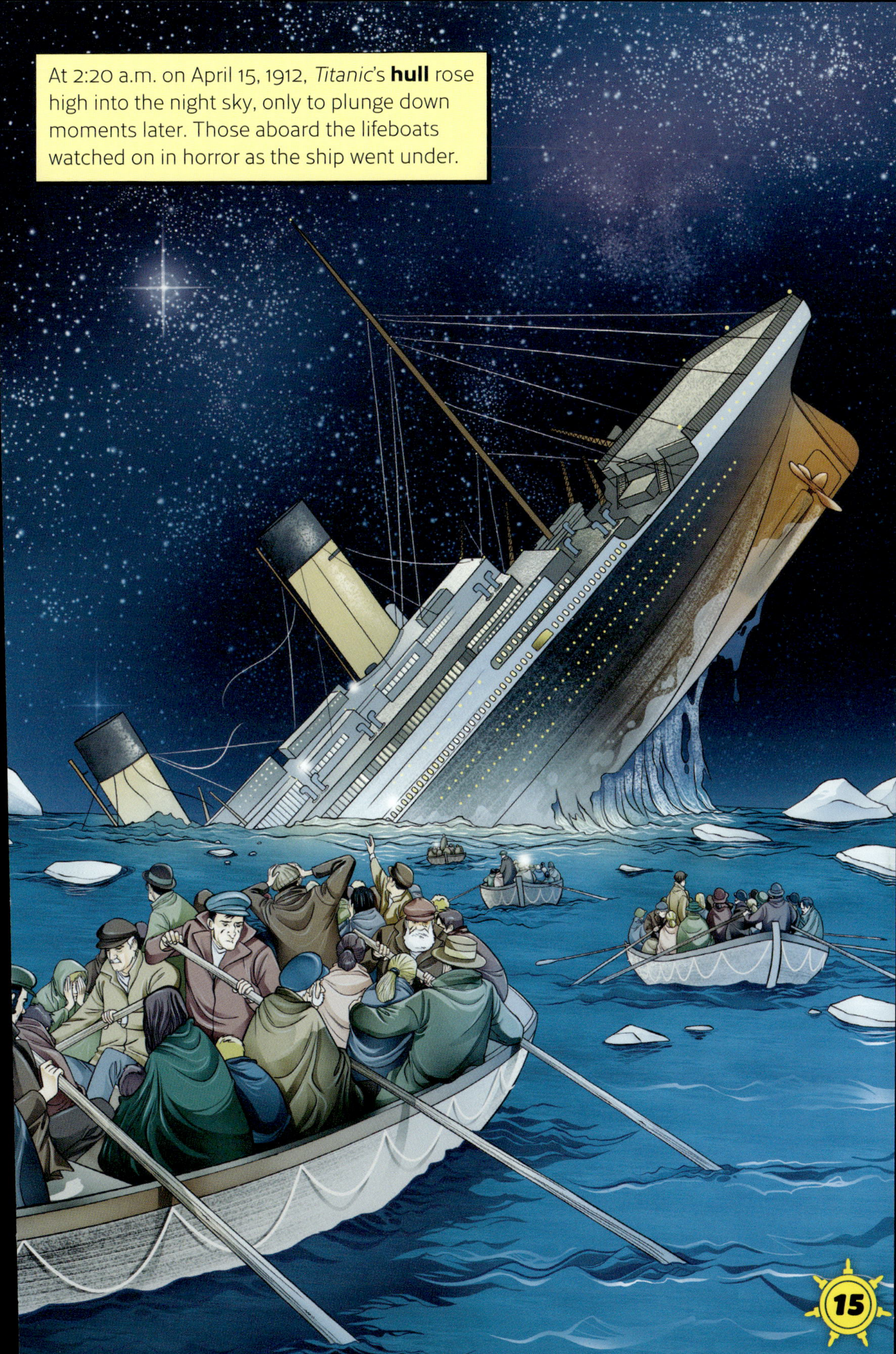
At 2:20 a.m. on April 15, 1912, *Titanic*'s **hull** rose high into the night sky, only to plunge down moments later. Those aboard the lifeboats watched on in horror as the ship went under.

CHAPTER 4

Rescued

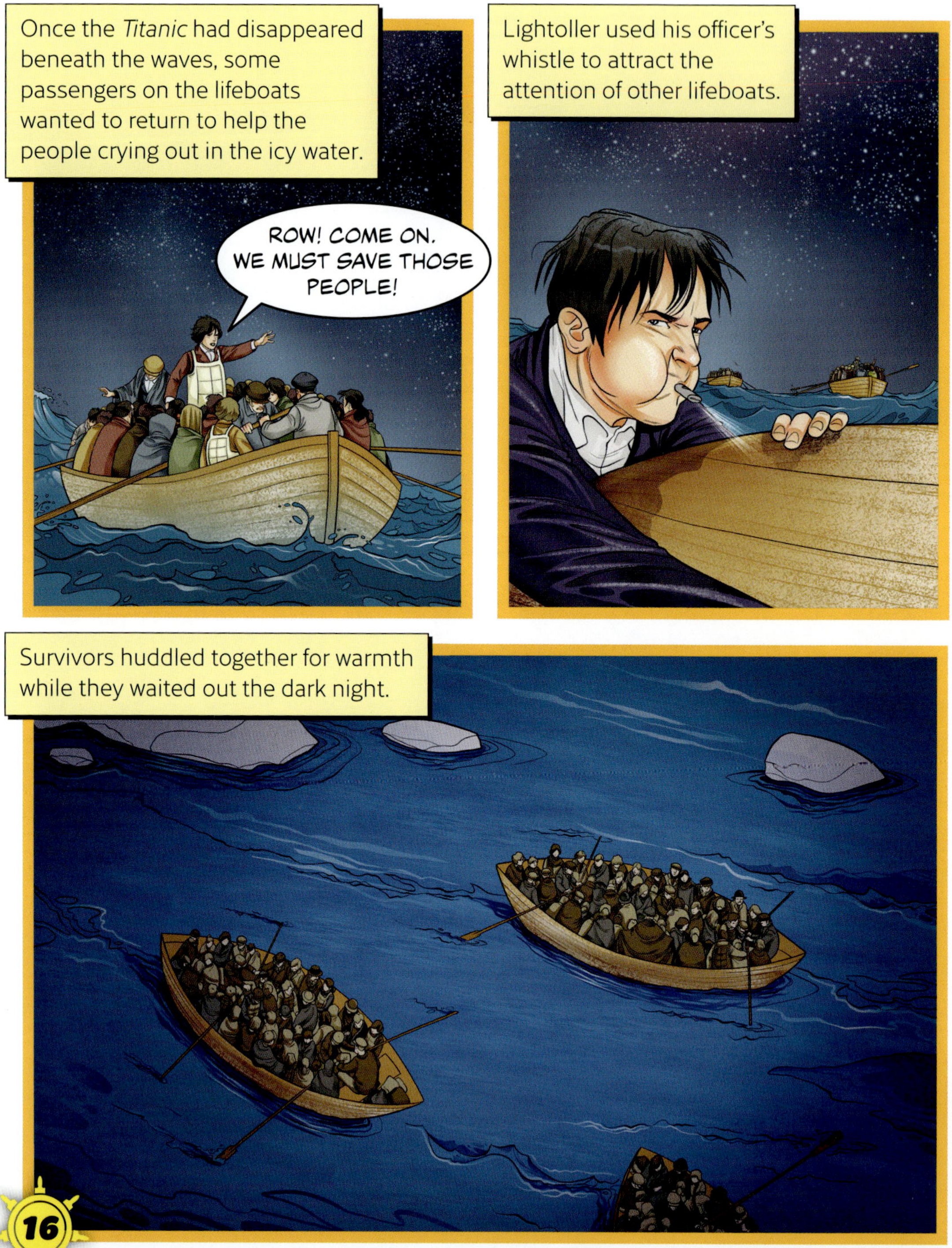
Once the *Titanic* had disappeared beneath the waves, some passengers on the lifeboats wanted to return to help the people crying out in the icy water.
ROW! COME ON. WE MUST SAVE THOSE PEOPLE!
Lightoller used his officer's whistle to attract the attention of other lifeboats.
Survivors huddled together for warmth while they waited out the dark night.

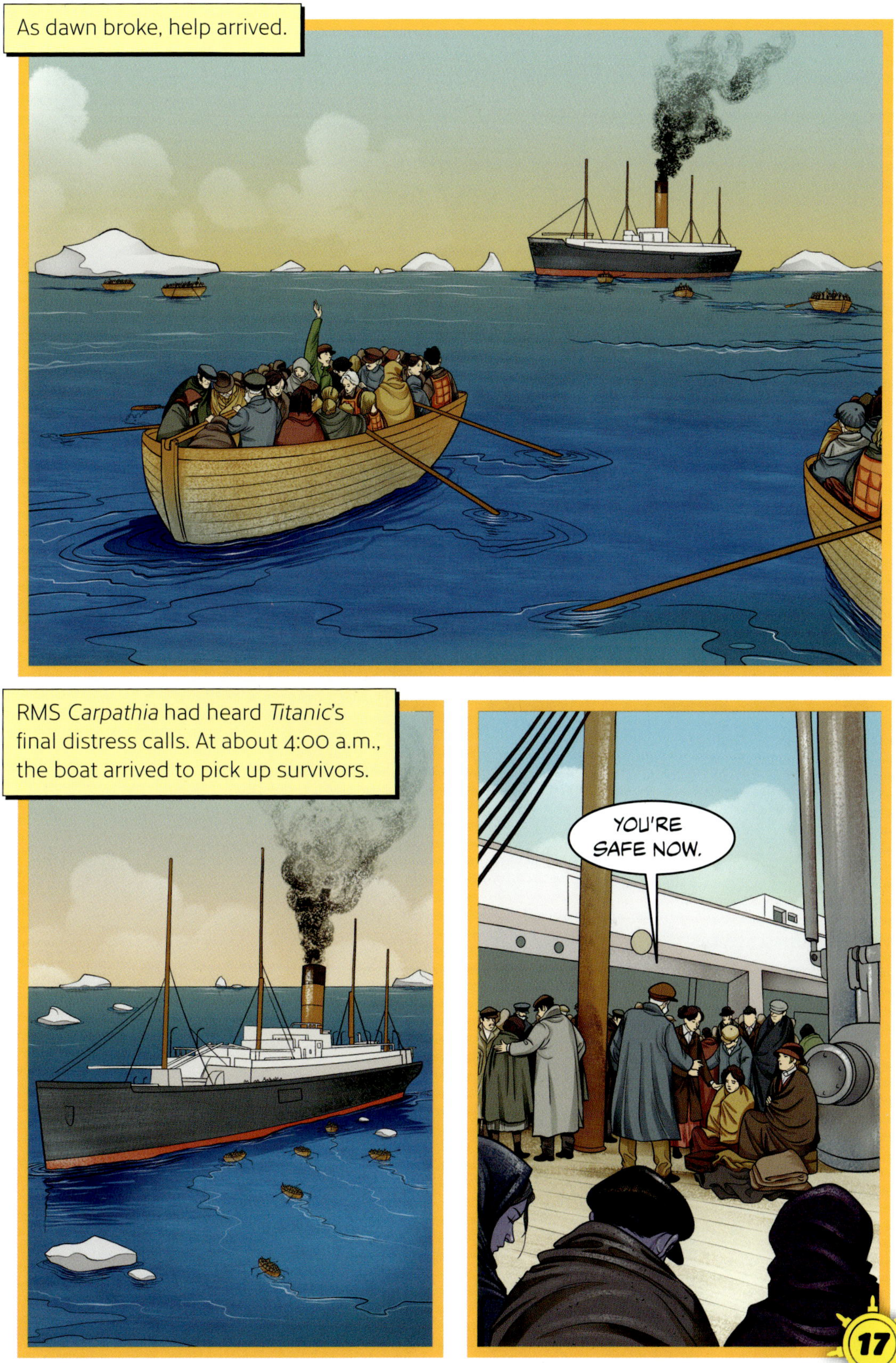
As dawn broke, help arrived.
RMS *Carpathia* had heard *Titanic*'s final distress calls. At about 4:00 a.m., the boat arrived to pick up survivors.
YOU'RE SAFE NOW.

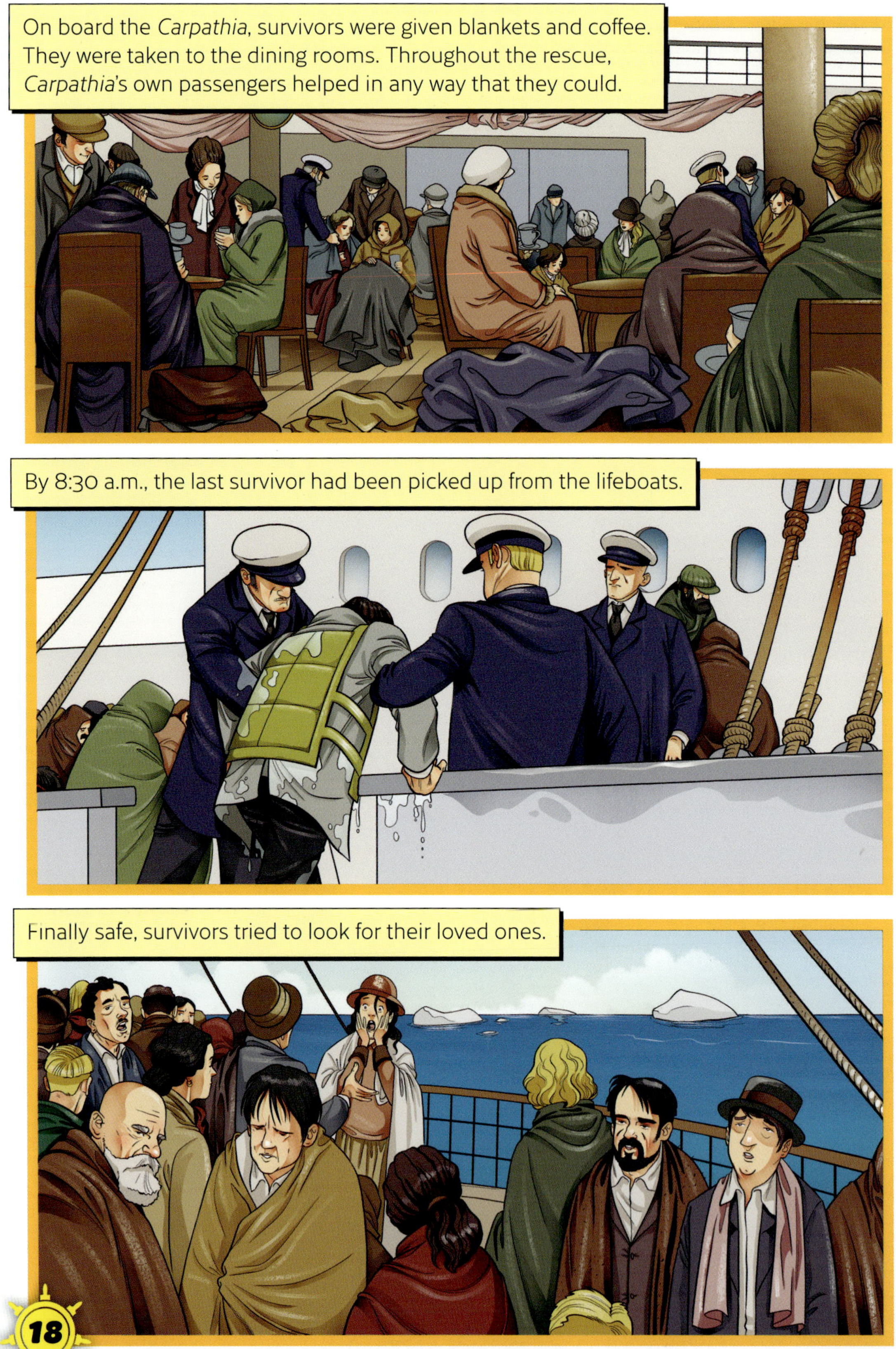
On board the *Carpathia*, survivors were given blankets and coffee. They were taken to the dining rooms. Throughout the rescue, *Carpathia*'s own passengers helped in any way that they could.
By 8:30 a.m., the last survivor had been picked up from the lifeboats.
Finally safe, survivors tried to look for their loved ones.

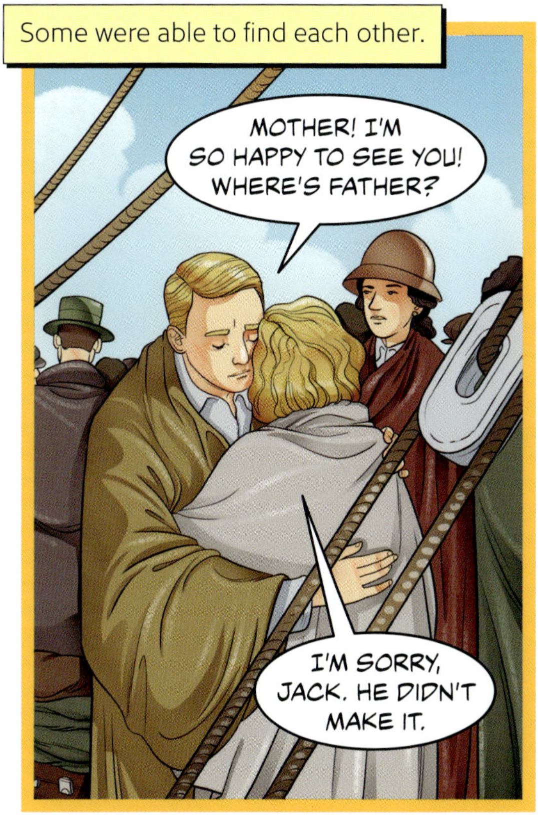
Some were able to find each other.
MOTHER! I'M SO HAPPY TO SEE YOU! WHERE'S FATHER?
I'M SORRY, JACK. HE DIDN'T MAKE IT.

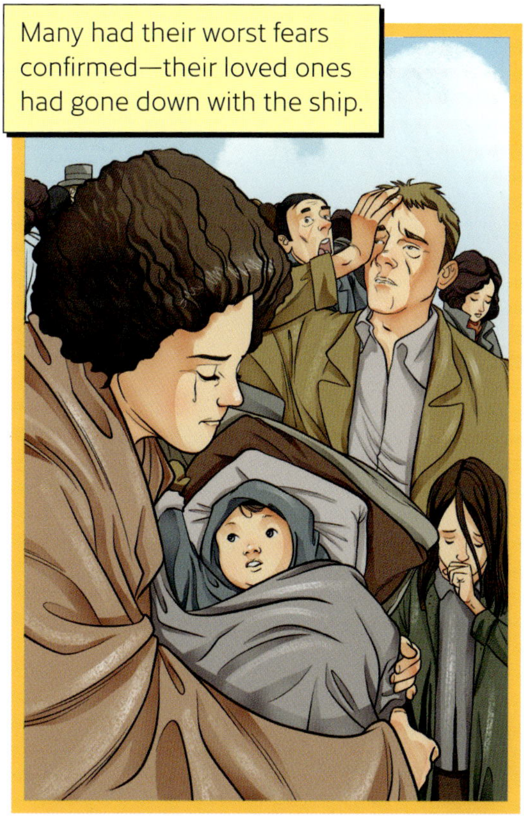
Many had their worst fears confirmed—their loved ones had gone down with the ship.

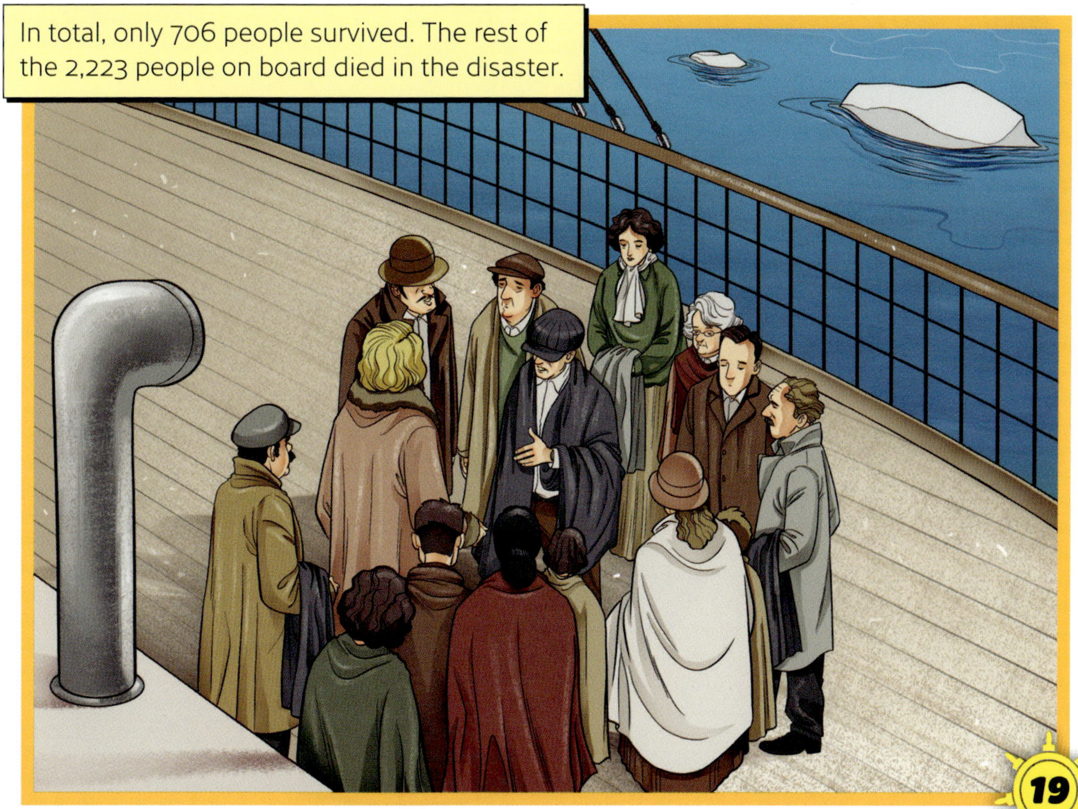
In total, only 706 people survived. The rest of the 2,223 people on board died in the disaster.

Lifesaving Measures

Titanic's lifeboats were stored on the ship's upper deck. At first, the massive ocean liner was supposed to carry 48 lifeboats—enough for everyone on board—but this number was reduced to 20 to give the deck a clearer view. In the end, that left space for only about half of the people on board. According to maritime law at the time, this was an acceptable amount, but a ship of this size had never been built before.

As the ship was sinking, passengers were instructed to put on life jackets. Women and children started boarding the lifeboats. Then, the crafts were lowered about 70 feet (20 m) down the side of the ship into the icy waters. Not all the crew had practiced this move, and some passengers felt the huge ship was safer than a tiny lifeboat. Only 28 people joined the first lifeboat, although it could hold 65. But as the ship began to tilt and sink, panic set in.

A VIEW OF SOME OF *TITANIC*'S LIFEBOATS ON THE SECOND-CLASS BOAT DECK

Titanic sent out distress calls to other ships in the area. The nearest ship, the SS *Californian*, didn't receive the message because their only telegraph operator had gone to bed. The first rescue ship to reach the scene —RMS *Carpathia*—took four hours. Only the lucky 706 people in the lifeboats survived.

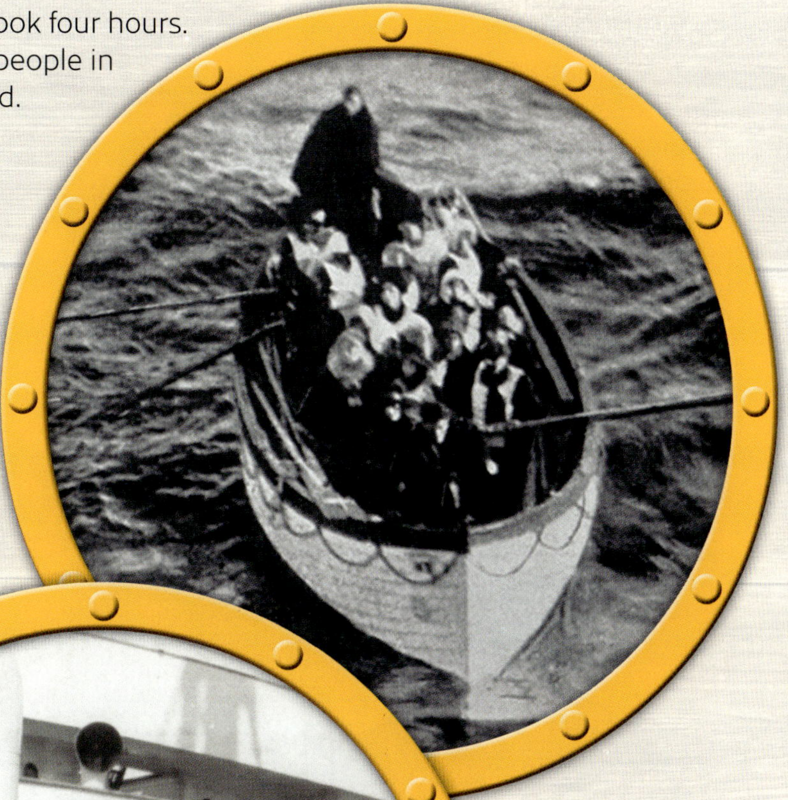

LIFEBOAT NUMBER 6 ON THE MORNING OF APRIL 15, CARRYING ONLY 24 PASSENGERS

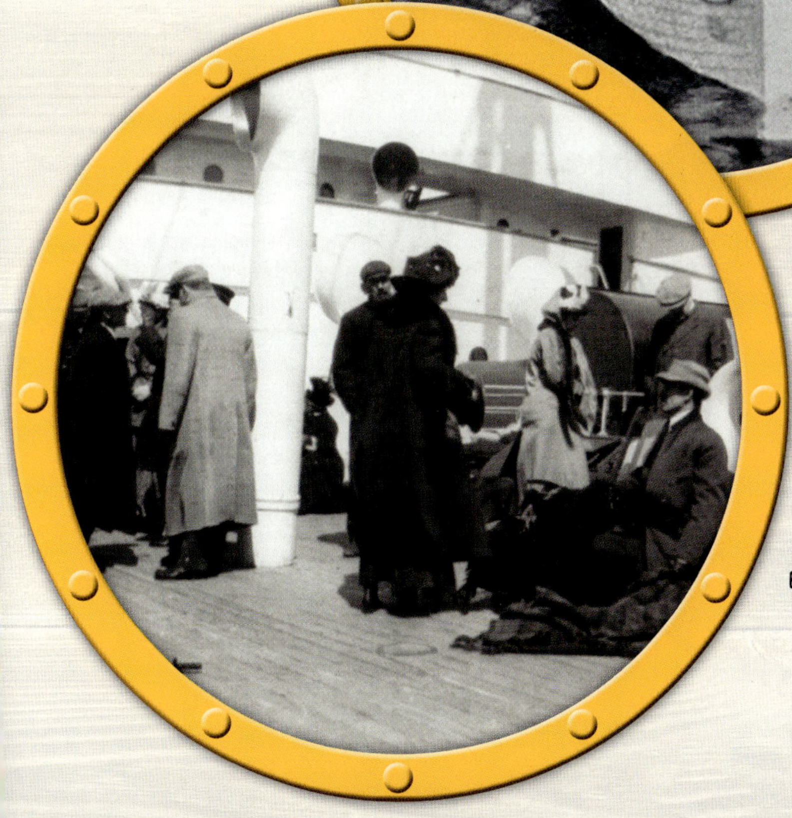

SURVIVORS ON BOARD THE RESCUE SHIP *CARPATHIA*

More Titanic Stories

Madeleine Astor was pregnant when she boarded *Titanic*. Her husband, John Jacob Astor IV, was one of America's wealthiest men, and the couple were returning from a long European honeymoon. Madeleine boarded lifeboat 4 and was rescued by RMS *Carpathia*. John asked to join his wife, given her condition, but he was ordered to stay on board. John's body was found in the Atlantic a week later. When their son was born, Madeleine named him John Jacob after his father.

JOHN JACOB ASTOR IV AND MADELEINE ASTOR

MARGARET BROWN

Margaret Brown was a first-class passenger on the *Titanic*. During the evacuation, Margaret was helping others board lifeboats when she was grabbed and thrown into lifeboat 6. As the boat was being launched with just 24 passengers, Margaret asked to turn back to search for more survivors, but a crew member refused. Margaret helped row her lifeboat, and when survivors boarded RMS *Carpathia* a few hours later, she continued to calm and care for her fellow passengers. She later set up a committee to help the survivors.

Glossary

bail to remove water from a boat or ship

erupted broke out suddenly and dramatically

evacuated removed from a place of danger to a safer place

fateful an important, often very bad, effect on future events

feat an achievement that requires great courage, skill, or strength

funnels chimneys on ships or steam engines

generators machines that turn mechanical energy into electrical energy

hull the main body of a ship, including the bottom, sides, and deck

ocean liner a large ship that can carry many people across the ocean

pumps devices that move liquid from one place to another

telegraph a system for sending long-distance messages, called telegrams

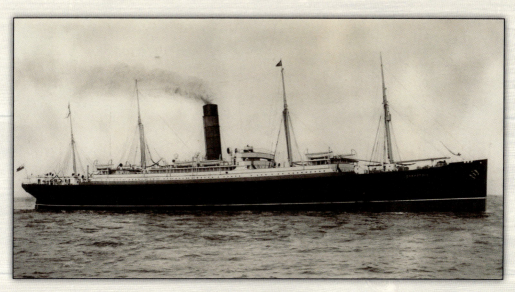

RMS CARPATHIA

Index

Astor, John and Madeleine 22
Brown, Margaret 22
Californian 21
Carpathia 17–18, 21–23
crew 7, 20, 22
Dean family 11
engineers 14
first-class passengers 6, 10, 16, 22
iceberg 4, 6
lifeboats 8–12, 15–16, 18, 20–22
Lightoller, Charles 12–13, 16
Straus, Isidor and Ida 10
telegraph 21
Thayer, Jack 6, 9, 19

Read More

McClure Anastasia, Laura. *Four Days on the* Titanic *(A True Book).* New York: Scholastic Inc., 2022.

O'Daly, Anne. *Sunken Ship of Dreams! The* Titanic, *1912 (Doomed History).* Minneapolis: Bearport Publishing Company, 2022.

Parkin, Michelle. *Atlantic Ocean Shipwrecks (Famous Shipwrecks).* Minneapolis: Jump!, Inc., 2024.

Learn More Online

1. Go to **FactSurfer.com** or scan the QR code below.
2. Enter "**Stories of Survival**" into the search box.
3. Click on the cover of this book to see a list of websites.